garden design for

OUTDOOR LIVING

Social Gatherings by Carson Arthur

Photographs by
Brendan Moffit
& Steve Lawrence

"Watch out, there's a new mood about…
which has very little to do with plant material
but everything to do with the nature of landscape."
– John Brookes

Published by CanWest Books Inc.
A subsidiary of CanWest MediaWorks Publications Inc.
1450 Don Mills Road
Toronto, ON
Canada, M3B 2X7

LIBRARY AND ARCHIVES CANADA CATALOGUING IN PUBLICATION

Arthur, Carson
    Garden design for outdoor living : social gatherings / Carson Arthur.

Includes index.

ISBN 0-9737410-1-5

    1. Gardens--Design. 2. Landscape gardening. I. Title.

SB473.A73 2006   712'.6   C2005-907557-0

Published in co-operation with AJE Productions Inc.

Edited by Meredith Birchall-Spencer
Photo Research by Alexander Aglialoro
Book Design by Fortunato Aglialoro / Fortunato Design Inc.

Printed and bound in Canada by Solisco

First Edition

10 9 8 7 6 5 4 3 2 1

Contents

Prologue

The gardens of today have changed from what they once were. No longer are our outdoor spaces planned around the grass, flowers, shrubs and trees that will occupy them. The emphasis today is on individuality. People want extensions of their homes, with usable features such as outdoor fireplaces, built-in kitchens and comfortable lounge seating. Spaces are designed around how they will be used on a daily basis. Low maintenance has become the driving force in current design—homeowners want gardens that look good and require little physical input because they just don't have the time to invest.

Homeowners want spaces that allow them to spend their weekends entertaining instead of maintaining. Once referred to in design circles as 'form follows function,' garden creators now have a new mantra: 'form follows life.' The harmony between the materials and different lifestyles is finally taking over from the drive to have different colour combinations of impatiens than your neighbour. More than ever, we now strive to satisfy the need to be as comfortable in our outdoor spaces as we are in our own homes.

In *Outdoor Living—Social Gatherings,* these gardens were designed for homeowners who had an idea of what they wanted, but were unsure of how to get it. Spaces have been rebuilt to meet today's ever-changing definition of the family, who are no longer willing to settle for the perennial-filled gardens of their grandparents. With a sense of adventure combined with a measure of balance, these gardens represent the homes of today. And even though each space is completely unique, they are each linked because they capture the same feeling—one of joy. These havens are for families where the priority was placed on the wellness of the spirit. No time for cutting grass or pulling weeds, their days are spent with loved ones restoring the soul for another week in the grind.

I hope that you will take inspiration from these gardens and realize the potential in your own space. I want you to become empowered to make changes in your own home so that it fits the lifestyle you want to live instead of the one you've grown accustomed to.

—CARSON ARTHUR

First Impressions

A Vancouver mansion's first impression wows them and a last impression leaves them wanting more.

Everyone knows that when a guest comes to your home, the front yard is the first thing that they see. What most people don't realize is that the front yard is also the last thing your guest remembers after that perfect dinner party. From bland to breathtaking, a front yard is reinvented.

Jane and Ron have worked hard for everything they have and they want a front yard that says successful, tasteful and established—all at once. After two decades of going to school, building careers as lawyers and starting a family, Jane and Ron have finally bought the home that they've always dreamed about. In one of the best neighbourhoods in Vancouver, across the street from several prestigious schools, this newly renovated mansion has it all—except for good landscaping. Jane and Ron need an outdoor space where they can greet guests, meet with business colleagues or just sit and read a book. They want all of this in the front, separate from the children's area out back.

Several years ago, Ron thought that stripping the old paint off of the front stairs would be a perfect weekend project. He lasted about an hour and the steps have looked the same ever since.

Dynamic in shape and structure, the top of their house on its corner lot can be seen above the 10-foot-tall hedge that surrounds the property. Unfortunately, the closer you get, the less appealing the view becomes. It's amazing when million-dollar homes have front yards that are nothing more then a lawn and a hedge. In this case, there is also an uneven concrete walkway and a set of painted stairs that have seen better days. A couple of huge yews hide the front door and a few tall evergreens represent the extent of mature plant life in this less than spectacular garden.

There is plenty of room to work with on this large lot. Replacing the walkway and fixing the stairs is an unfinished project of Ron's, who wants the entranceway to be safer for his elderly parents and but still look stylish. Jane also wants some privacy from their neighbour's home to the east. She envisions a space out of one of her gardening magazines, perfect in every detail.

DOs & DON'Ts

DON'T ignore the front of your home. Most neighbourhoods are full of front yards with nothing but grass and some foundation plantings. Create drama with some low-maintenance architectural items like large cement balls or sculptured metal trellises. Add impact by painting the door such rich dark colours as red and chocolate brown. Aim for a front yard that people stop to look at as they pass.

DO incorporate planters into your design. Urns that flank the door add a formal, yet personal flair, to the front of your home. Use your own creativity in planting spring bulbs in March, stunning perennials in June, flowering kale in September and arranging dogwood twigs and evergreen boughs for those winter days. Not only will your guests be impressed, the planters will also make you smile after a long day at work.

DO have seating near the door. There are two very good reasons for having a bench at the front door. It's a great place to have coffee in the morning as you watch the neighbourhood wake up and you have somewhere to sit and talk to those unexpected guests when the inside of your house is not at its best.

Currently, the large front yard is used as a soccer field, a badminton court and a driving range. A front yard should be an expression of the inside of a home. It's meant to be personable and inviting, so that when guests arrive at the door, they have an idea of who lives here.

The new design includes the widening of the path to accommodate more than one guest, a screened area for quiet seating safe from flying soccer balls and a large arbour to add structure and height. The arbour also creates height so that it doesn't feel like the house towers above the front yard. Matching screens provide privacy along the eastern edge of the property while lush gardens give visual texture and link the elements.

Plan

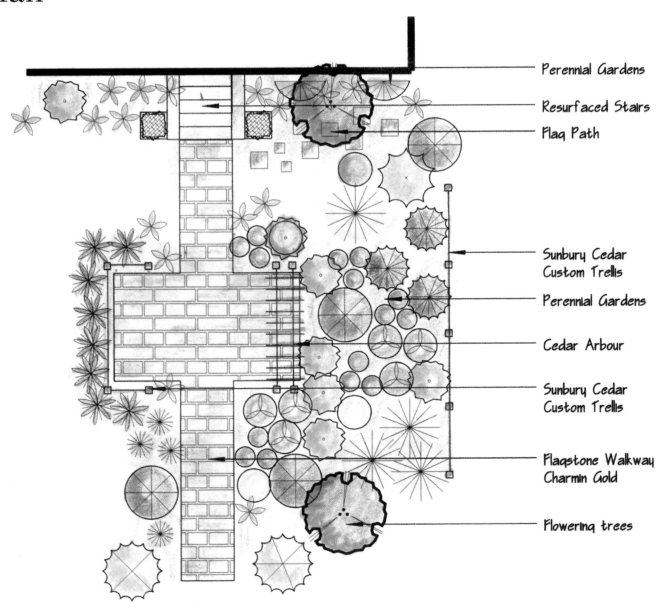

Perennial Gardens

Resurfaced Stairs

Flag Path

Sunbury Cedar Custom Trellis

Perennial Gardens

Cedar Arbour

Sunbury Cedar Custom Trellis

Flagstone Walkway Charmin Gold

Flowering trees

Materials

The front stairs are a good size and shape and require only a facelift. Slate tile is ideal for resurfacing the steps—it's rough enough to provide traction on wet days and hardy enough to handle the elements. This particular tile was chosen to make the grey tones of the house work with all of the brown tones used in the rest of the garden.

Custom-designed cedar trellises provide vertical elements to the space and help alleviate the sense that the house and the garden are perpendicular to each other. The flat lawn no longer meets the flat side of the house. Jane and Ron have the choice to seal the wood to keep the warm brown tones, or leave it untreated so that the cedar will age to match the silver grey tones in the house.

The caramel rich tones of this Charmin Gold flagstone make the garden warm and enveloping. While a geometric pattern may have been a better complement to the house, this particular stone is only available in natural shapes. To make the rock work with the lines of the home, an architectural focal point will be added to the centre of the walkway.

Vancouver nurseries are full of specimens that make true gardeners drool and because Vancouver's climate is perfect for almost everything, selection is unlimited. Jane collects gardening books, so we gave her collectable plants. While the plants in her garden need to be dramatic and colourful, they also have to be low maintenance because even though she knows quality, Jane admits she has no time to tend to the space.

opposite: Beauty Berry—*Callicarpa japonica*

clockwise from top: Winter Jasmine—*Jasminium nudiflorum*, Coreopsis—*Coreopsis auriculata 'Zagreb'*, Golden Ninebark—*Physocarpus opulifolius 'Dart's Gold'*, Bluebeard—*Caryopteris incana*, Cypress—*Chamaecyparis obtusa*

ARBOURS vs PERGOLAS

Both the terms arbour and pergola are used to describe a structure that encloses a space. Designed to support vines, trees or flowers, both arbours and pergolas are essential in landscape design. The major difference between the two is how you use it. If you sit under it, then it's an arbour; if you walk through it, it's a pergola.

right: *Our furniture stylist Patti Ransom adds panache to this Vancouver garden.*

below: *The dark tones in the resin-wicker and the natural stripes in the cushions work well with the multiple colours in the flagstone.*

Although often limited in quantity, the furniture at the front of the home has to be functional as well as beautiful. As an accessory, a design element or just a place to set the groceries, the furniture is crucial in setting the tone and feel. Here, two contained seating areas not only create impact, they also provide Jane with a place to perch and admire her new garden.

We don't often consider front yards as places to entertain, but when we understand how the space is used, we begin to realize that they are in fact for social gatherings. Jane and Ron now have a garden worthy of their home. The addition of cedar trellises give the garden shape: planted with jasmine, the trellises wrap the space with texture and structure while creating privacy.

Unique flagstone paths lead through the garden, past quaint spots for sitting, and up to a dramatic set of stairs. Flanked by large cedar-filled urns, the front door now has the proper proportions for a home of this magnitude. Guests and neighbours are now welcomed by an inviting space. This home has become worthy of its corner lot in such a high-end borough and the garden is now the envy of the neighbourhood instead of the embarrassment.

A Fresh Approach

A modern approach to an urban yard for a contemporary family.

Designing a city garden for a young family is always a challenge. These gardens are the origin of the term 'postage stamp'. Not only do they need to be an effective use of all of the space in a tight area, they also have to meet the needs of each family member who lives there.

With two careers and their first child, Riley, time for homeowner's Anne and Mike is at a premium. The garden design has to be contemporary, uncluttered and easy to maintain. They want to spend their weekends on long bike rides, playing in the park or shopping at the market; the last thing they need is a yard that ties them down.

opposite: *This add-on land hung like an afterthought off the back of the garden. The leftover bit between two homes in the back, this piece of property ended up belonging to Anne and Mike. Without a purpose, it became a home for weeds.*

This home posed some great challenges. The first being the several types of brick that visually dominated the small space. With this many patterns and colours, the eye is overwhelmed. Removing much of this confusion was a priority.

Another challenge was the layout of the yard. The lot had a unique 10-by-15-foot plot attached to the rear corner, which emphasized the fact that the homes at the back of the property stood higher than the garden, making for interesting privacy issues.

Anne and Mike's garden needed a lot of work. In fact, it required a complete overhaul. All of the shades of red and brown had to work together and, at the same time, disappear. A new patio—attached to the back of the home, not six feet into the yard like the existing one—big enough to hold a table, the barbecue and a lounge chair for reading was essential. Riley needed a space to be play and Mom and Dad needed a place for themselves. The extra bit of property at the back had to be tied into the garden so it felt like one complete space.

Plan

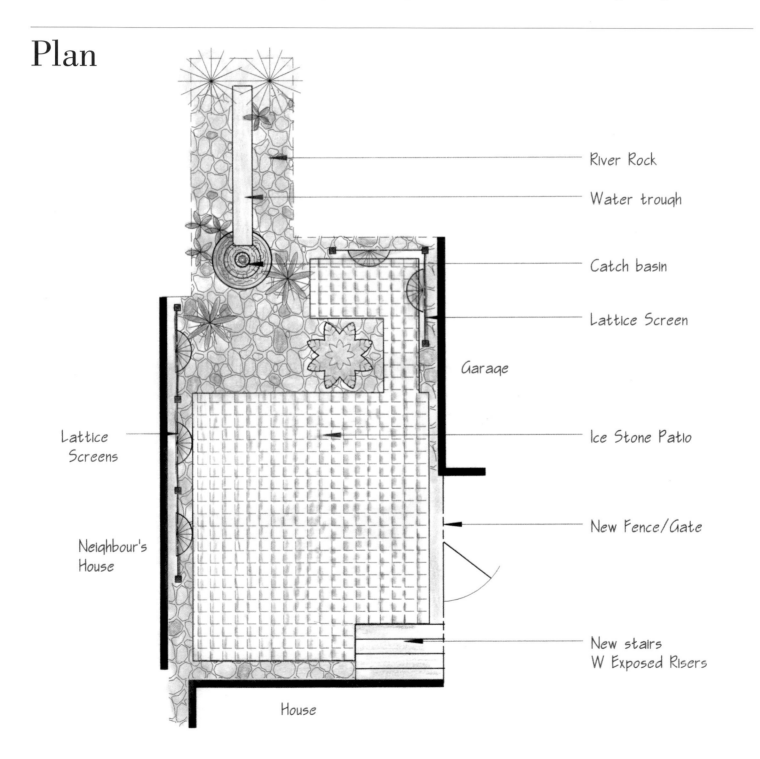

River Rock

Water trough

Catch basin

Lattice Screen

Garage

Lattice Screens

Ice Stone Patio

Neighbour's House

New Fence/Gate

New stairs W Exposed Risers

House

Materials

Beach pebbles replaced mulch in between the plants as a low-maintenance ground cover. It creates texture and depth without having empty spaces in the plant beds. To ensure that weeds wouldn't grow between the stones, a specially designed filter cloth was placed between the plants. Porous enough for water to pass, the cloth works as a barrier between the weeds and the soil.

The lattice panels erected around the perimeter of the garden, in the same reddish-brown colour as the brick, served two purposes. One consistent colour wrapping around the entire space allowed the eye to notice the garden before the surrounding walls and it hid the yard from the neighbour's sightlines.

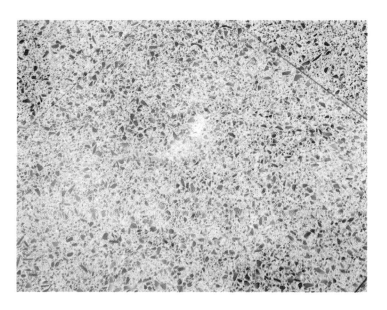

How to surface the patio became an important decision. The surrounding space was made up of strong colours and bold patterns that could not be changed. The patio needed to be made of a material that would complement the existing elements and not compete with them. A new product called IceStone—a custom mix of recycled glass blended with concrete—was used to form large tiles. It brought together all of the red tones in the space, while providing a surface that stretched from one side of the yard to the other. *Tip:* When ordering this product for yourself, provide the manufacturer with the colours you want to match, and they can create something just for you.

DOs & DON'Ts

DO create separate areas for adults and children. It is important for everyone to feel as if they have a place in the garden. Too often parents concede the back-yard to the kids. Even this small backyard, providing a space that will grow with Riley was a priority. By incorporating an elevation change and a planting bed, Riley's play area is clearly defined.

DO take advantage of spaces that are unique. In this case, it was the terraced area at the back. Through the creation of a custom piece of artwork, Anne and Mike have a conversation-starting water feature. A wise person once said, 'imagination is always free.' Expend a little brainpower and come up with something that no else has.

This is a one-of-a-kind water feature. A Plexi-glass trough starts in the formerly unused back corner, drawing the eye away from the extra patch of land and into the centre of the new garden.

WATERWORKS

Water features serve three main purposes in a garden. First and foremost, they are attractive. People like water in a garden whether it's moving or still. Another reason we use water is for the sound. The bubbling, gurgling noises are a perfect mask for the din of city living such as automobile and playground ruckus. The third reason for having water is as a lure for wildlife. Birds, squirrels and deer give a magical air to the garden that is very hard to artificially introduce.

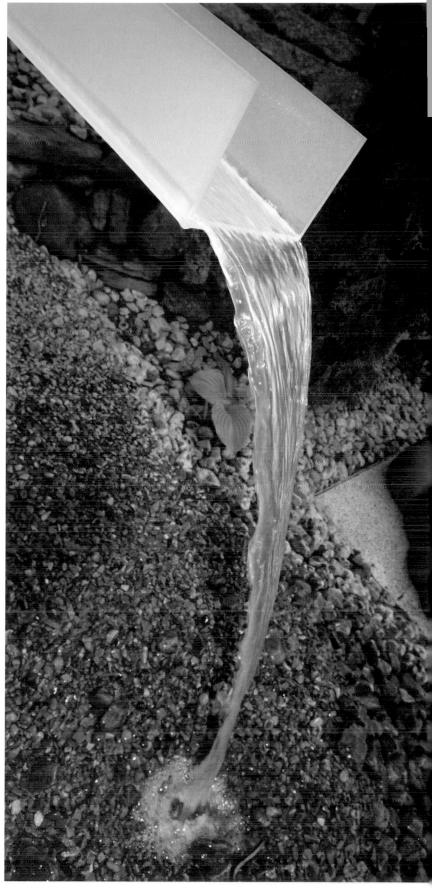

This was a tough garden for plants to flourish in because of the conditions: half was in a sandy, shaded area and the other half sat in full sun with rocky soil. Ferns, Lily of the Valley, and Brunnera found homes in the beds of the most shaded areas and river rock and plants such as Princess Lily and Serviceberry were planted in the sun-filled beds. We wanted to imitate the habitats of dry river beds and forest glades so we planted specimens that are naturally found in those environments, with a few exceptions.

opposite: Purple-leafed Sand Cherry—*Prunus x cistena*

right: Lily of the Valley—*Convallaria majalis*
bottom: Jack Frost Brunnera—*Brunnera macrophylla*

With so many browns and reds in the backyard, putting vibrancy and life back into this space had to be accomplished with bold, bright primary colours. This was the garden of a twenty-something couple and the design had to be hip and stylish and, at the same time, practical and efficient.

right: *Michelle Mawby was brought on board to select the furniture for this garden.*

below: *To give Anne flexibility in her outdoor space, bold colours were only introduced in the accessories, which can be easily updated for every season.*

This garden became the perfect place for a young urban couple because it combined all things a new family needed. With the new enlarged patio, dinner and drinks with guests will never again be a balancing act and an area designated just for kids keeps them from getting underfoot.

No longer is this a disjointed and disconnected backyard. The lattice panels and the recycled glass tiles have minimized the browns and reds and the vibrant colours of the accessories and the children's toys give the eye a new focus.

We changed the sightlines uniting with garden with a new Plexi-glass water feature extending from the wasted section in the back to the edge of the patio. Bright colours and hardy plants are perfect accessories to a space designed for urban living.

Modern Classic

From tea and crumpets to scotch on the rocks: a masculine makeover for the modern man.

Transforming an urban space that was perfect for a little old lady into a backyard hip enough for a contemporary guy is a classic design dilemma. Here, a fussy, flower-filled yard is redesigned to be sleek, stylish and sexy.

above: *Carmen's second storey window offers a great view of the yard.*
below: *The flagstone path divides the yard in two, creating two separate and competing spaces versus a single complete unit.*

Carmen is an admitted perfectionist with a charming smile and an effervescent attitude and he expects his home and garden to reflect his personality: well-dressed, well-spoken and well-organized. He wants a space that makes him happy when he arrives home from a busy day. His garden needs to be orderly and structured and, at the same time, natural and untamed; rugged materials combined with clean, sophisticated lines. Carmen's perfect backyard should impress his guests, whether he's hosting a catered event or a simple barbecue. No run-of-the-mill yard will do—Carmen wants a posh garden to complement his taste for the finer things in life.

The stairs were wide enough for only one person, which was dangerous in the rain and snow or when carrying large items and groceries.

With English-style plant beds teeming with perennials, lattice panels and random flagstone pathways; the backyard was adorable but muddled and didn't reflect Carmen's style. The original garden was not designed to maximize the space. Without a proper patio or seating, this small yard was nothing more then a pretty place to pass through. Carmen was embarrassed to have friends sit on the tiny, uneven collection of stones and the diminutive deck had limited useable space and its stairs were clearly not functional in size or location. The best parts of this backyard were the plants and, as a closet gardener, Carmen wanted to keep and looked forward to maintaining them. Ultimately, he was looking for a clean, contemporary, well-ordered jungle.

opposite: *Many of the garden's existing flowers were just too feminine for Carmen's taste.*

The first priority for this garden was the design of a patio. The plan featured a 500-square-foot circular, natural flagstone patio. Rarely seen in gardens, circles are a dramatic attention-grabbing element. The patio had to be large enough to become the dominant focal point in the small yard and by placing it in the centre the area seems much larger because the eye is immediately drawn to the point farthest away from each property line. The circular theme continues in a show-stopping water feature beside the redesigned deck. The random flagstone from the old garden is recycled to form paths linking the garage and stairs to the patio. Plants were also added to the gardens to create four seasons of interest, while existing plants were relocated for balance.

Plan

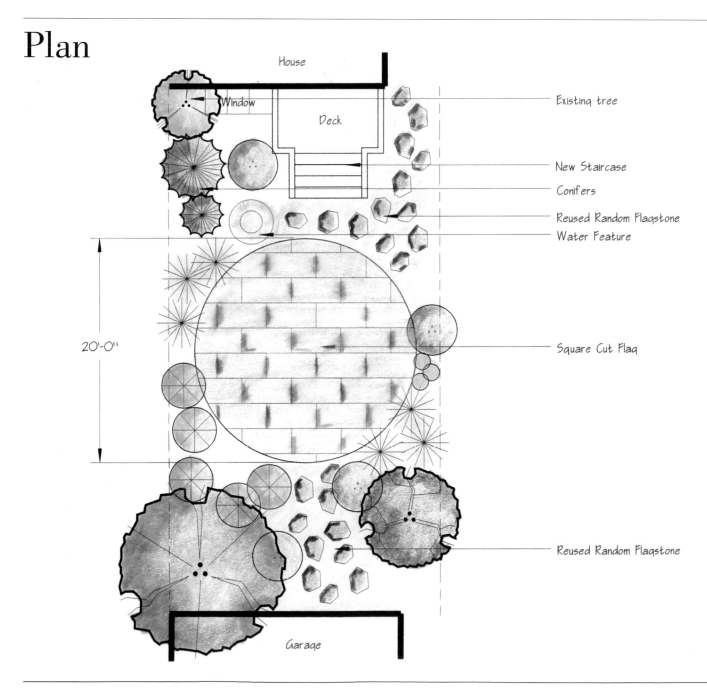

House

Window

Deck

Existing tree

New Staircase

Conifers

Reused Random Flagstone

Water Feature

20'-0"

Square Cut Flag

Reused Random Flagstone

Garage

DOs & DON'Ts

DO mix classical elements into a modern garden. When living in an older style home (in a Georgian or Victorian for example) having a garden that is too modern looks out of place. Most people who are attracted to modern gardens enjoy the clean lines, the mix of elements and the juxtaposition of materials. But you can often successfully marry the two extremes. Using antiques such as rusted statuary, obelisks and trellises in a modern setting allows for interplay in the space and creates a harmony between the home and the garden. They act as a transition between the two design principles.

DON'T underestimate the size of your stairs. Stairs should not be less then three-and-a-half feet wide: the perfect width for one person, but wide enough for two people to pass comfortably. How steep the stairs are is also very important when deciding the dimensions. The height and depth of a normal step is at least 12-inches-deep by six-to-eight-inches-tall. We all climb stairs everyday and we immediately notice when we are walking on something different: sometimes this is good, but most times it is bad.

SMALL SPACE TRICK

Create visual depth in a small garden with the use of mirrors. They trick the eye into thinking that the garden is twice its actual size. With many varieties of outdoor mirrors available, they have also become affordable for the average homeowner. A word of caution, however, when using these highly reflective devices. To make a mirror look less obvious on a fence or a wall, plants are often placed in front of it to blur the edges. While esthetically this is a great idea, we forget that a mirror reflects sunlight as well and the backside of the plant will burn from the intense brightness. If you plan to try this at home, use plants that have grey foliage like Lamb's Ear Stachys byzantina, as they are able to handle the heat.

Materials

In this city garden, water is used to reduce the hum of busy neighbours and the local traffic. Here, a fantastic fountain, shaped like a water bowl, has a contemporary look and complements the circular patio design. Filled with water in the summer, this fountain does double-duty as a planter that holds evergreen bough, and twinkle lights in the winter.

Natural stone is arguably the most beautiful patio material. However, natural stone that is cut on the sides—square cut—is often a better choice for creating level seating surfaces because the joints between stones are smaller. A chair leg or the heel of a shoe is less likely to slip through a tight seam between the stones. Here, a dark grey tone adds masculinity and draws the eye to the yard's centre.

In a modern garden, vibrant colours are best captured in the accessories. Hot pink is introduced through annuals in bronze-coloured zinc containers. This way, the homeowner can update with fresh choices every season. When colour is used in permanent materials like stone, it will remain the same for the life of the space.

With sun, shade and an enthusiastic gardener, plant choices are wide open. Flora was chosen for uniqueness. However, these are not the plants for the timid and are best grown by someone who knows how to maintain them. With their invasive and temperamental nature, they can quickly overtake a small space.

opposite: Katsura—*Cercidiphyllum japonicum*

right: Peony—*Paeonia emodi*
below: Scabiosa—*Scabiosa minoana*

Opposites attract, even in a garden. Modern furniture can be combined with rugged elements to create a harmonious relationship. Here, the clarity of the large stone patio sets the stage for furniture that is masculine but refined, so it doesn't overwhelm the small space. Rich tones mixed with polished metals provide pizzazz and the various textures add complexity. Modern influences combine with classic styles to increase the garden's adaptability.

right: *Carson chats with Scott McCuaig, the person responsible for the furniture selections.*
bottom left: *Rocks strategically placed at the base of the large tree enrich the look of the yard.*

This garden has become sleek, stylish and sexy. Carmen now has a place to entertain guests or wind down after a busy day. Perfect for Carmen's inner gardener, each plant provides a new challenge. More importantly, the plants now add four seasons of interest to a space that lacked winter personality.

The yard feels much bigger, even though more space is now occupied. The original lawn was sacrificed in favour of a bigger patio to accommodate large parties or intimate gatherings. Serviceable and visually interesting, pathways and wide stairs allow for freedom of movement between the house and the garage.

This is exactly what Carmen asked for: a spot perfect for martinis with friends.

A Gardener's Gallery

From a summer joyride to a four season journey; a gardener's creation goes on a trip of reinvention.

Flowerbeds full of summer-blooming perennials get some company as one woman's passion evolves from plain to perfect—a masterpiece fit for an art gallery.

Marlene and Howard represent a landscape designer's toughest challenge. He is a doctor and works every day with minute details and precision; she is a true gardener with affiliations with horticultural clubs and garden groups. Together, they have high expectations of what their backyard renovation should look like. They will settle for nothing less.

Marlene has spent years assembling a fantastic arrangement of flowering perennials. Full of colours and textures, her garden is the envy of her neighbours, yet Marlene isn't satisfied. She is tired of looking at nothing during the winter and wants varieties of plants and shrubs that will give her four seasons of interest.

Howard is only allowed in the backyard to cut the grass. Howard wants to invade on his wife's territory; he wants less grass and more space for himself and a neutral area that they both can enjoy.

opposite: *Even the back of a flower can be stunning.*

Many of Marlene's plants were worth saving. They just needed to be moved to new locations in the garden.

below: Gloriosa Daisy—*Rudbeckia 'Maxine'*
right: Cedar—*Thuja occidentalis*

The original garden was a collection of pretty flowers, planted layer upon layer and pushed up against the cedar privacy hedges. On three sides, the flowerbeds frame the lawn, which is adjacent to a small interlock patio that foots the sliding doors.

While the yard is medium-sized, the plant beds clearly define the proportions of the space. Nothing is left to the imagination here, as everything is very straightforward. As beautiful as the flowers may be, the view from any position in the garden is the same. Everything has its place and is in control. There is one major obstacle that Howard and Marlene must contend with: an extremely large apartment building looks directly down into their yard. The neighbouring building was their first home together and even though they have fond memories, Marlene and Howard would definitely like to see less of it.

Clearly this space has been loved, but with no definition or focal point, the eye wanders from plant to plant.

The first stage in this garden renovation is to remove almost everything from the space, including the little patio, most of the grass and all of Marlene's perennials. Although the plants are being reused, their placement allows the beds to be opened up to make room for some shrubs and trees. A new, larger patio will give Howard a much-needed space in the yard, far enough away from the flowers for Marlene's comfort level. A privacy arbour frames the patio and a water feature anchors the back right corner of the garden. A French garden with a Versailles theme is employed to add impact and drama. Several concrete statues and an arch mimic the arbour and give height to the formerly one-dimensional layout.

Plan

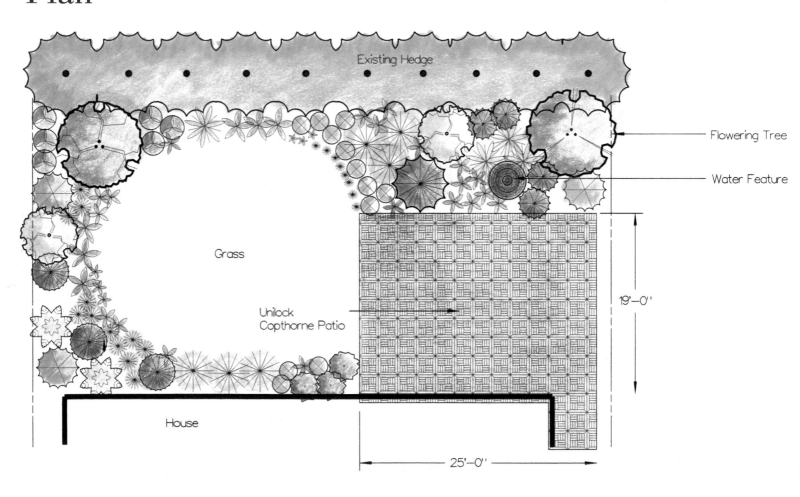

Existing Hedge

Flowering Tree

Water Feature

Grass

Unilock
Copthorne Patio

House

19'-0''

25'-0''

A red brick house is one of the hardest to complement when building a patio because few patio stones match the deep claret and rust tones found in the bricks. A new concrete formed stone called Copthorne, made in Belgium, was selected for its colour and versatility. Each patio stone is a replica of the bricks found on Marlene and Howard's home.

below: *No one less than David Copperfield was going to make that apartment building disappear. Putting a visual distraction between it and the garden's occupants would alleviate the problem though. Here, a dramatic arbour does the trick. With rafters on a 30-degree angle, eight feet above the ground, the arbour demands notice. When sitting at the patio table, people are still aware of the building, but it is no longer the first thing they see. In time, the Virginia creeper planted at the base will find its ways up the columns and across the rafters, partially obscuring the view.*

Materials

To reduce some of the white noise created from the adjacent buildings and parking lots, a dramatic fountain was introduced into the garden. Selected for its striking shape, this spherical orb creates just enough water flow to muffle the nearby car sounds. It also draws birds into the space and acts as a conversation piece for visitors.

DOs & DON'Ts

DON'T place low growing flowerbeds at the extreme perimeters of a yard. The focal point becomes the seam where the exterior fence meets the lawn and not the beds themselves. Visually, the eye is drawn to the spot where the horizontal meets the vertical planes and it skips past all of the good stuff in between. To fix this problem, layer your plant beds so that the tallest growing ones are in the back. Visually, the flowers should look like they slope from the front upwards to the back making the space feel bigger, and blurring the horizontal plane.

DO plant wooded shrubs and evergreens among your perennial beds. In regions with long winters, creating visual interest that stays around after the snow has fallen is often underrated. Choose shrubs that have unique branch colours or shapes. Cork Screw Hazel, for example, looks great with a light snowfall to highlight each curve of every branch. Evergreens also easily fix the winter blahs because they virtually stay the same for all four seasons. Try some of the blue junipers to add a colour other than green.

GARDEN ART

Bring out your old and rusted pieces of garden art because old is definitely new again. Patina is the buzzword when it comes to found objects. If something has character, or loosely translated: if it looks like it has been through the ringer once or twice, then you want it in your garden. Be careful of going down this road though, there is a fine line between hip and trendy and over-the-top kitsch. A few pieces are a delight; too many are a yard sale.

While Marlene had a huge selection of plants, her collection lacked those that lend height, winter interest or late-fall colour. But because she's a gardener, new additions were chosen even though they are high maintenance.

Shrubs were placed between the low-growing perennials and the cedar hedge, to provide the garden depth. Low-growing evergreens such as Junipers, break up the band of flowers, while grasses such as Miscanthus, were introduced to increase Marlene's compilation.

clockwise from top:
Rose Mallow—*Hibiscus 'Lord Baltimore'*
Rose of Sharon—*Hibiscus syriacus*
Gloriosa Daisy—*Rudbeckia 'Maxine'*

opposite:
Engelman's Virginia Creeper—*Parthenocissus quinquefolia*

This garden used to be orderly but bland, with the introduction of several dramatic statues, we gave it some personality. Like its older and more regal cousin, Versailles, this backyard needed a blend of concrete and iron furniture that would withstand the worst winter can throw at it. The new patio provides ample space for dinner parties and horticultural meetings and provides Howard a spot where he can just sit back and watch Marlene hard at work.

Ernst Hupel, Marlene's interior designer and the person responsible for all of the finishing touches in this tribute to French garden design.

In most gardens today, plants are accessories, sidelined to make room for big lawns, patios and pools; but here, the plants are front and centre because Marlene spends hours lovingly tending each and every bush, branch, and bloom and it shows. Spring, summer, winter or fall, this garden now has something for Marlene to enjoy.

The renovated yard pays homage to Marlene's passion. By increasing the size of the beds and adding new focal points, Marlene has a backyard designed to be an art gallery for her creations where she and her guests can sit and soak it all in. With less lawn and a bigger patio, Howard gets exactly what he was seeking, a private and restful refuge from his busy practise.

Big Sky Garden

Making a dull and lifeless garden into a space good enough for a country boy, his daughter and his wife, a two-time Olympic gold medallist.

They say that home is where the heart is, but what happens when your house is in the city, and your soul is in the country? Take the best of both worlds and make them work in a single space.

After a phenomenal speed skating career, Catriona [Lemay Doan] retired from the sport

in 2003 and had her first child, Greta. With a busy schedule as both a mom and a sports commentator, she shares her familial duties with her husband Bart, a true cowboy. On weekends, Bart competes in rodeos with his horse. He loves being at the farm, but their home is in the city, perfect for Catriona who still travels for work and public speaking engagements. So, they want a space that is low maintenance, has all of the amenities of living in the city but also one that captures the spirit of those wide-open spaces that Bart loves so much.

The two-person table may have been enough when it was just Bart and Catriona, but now Greta makes three, so it will be set aside in favour of something larger.

With the original old shed, a weathered fire pit and a cement slab patio, the backyard is shockingly bland for a young family with so much personality. Besides the strollers for jogging and the surplus of toys, the only new addition to the yard is the hottub, much needed when the rodeo doesn't go as planned.

Catriona wants a backyard that meets her growing family's needs: a place for Greta, a separate area for entertaining and lots of colourful flowers. Bart's biggest concern is that in fulfilling all their needs, the area will seem smaller. The challenge will be to combine all the new large elements into the medium-sized urban backyard, while keeping the space from feeling crowded. The garden has to be both multipurpose and safe. In addition to more storage, the couple also wants a patio and a space that feels more like 50 acres than a metropolitan-sized postage stamp. They need a garden designed to harmonize these two extremes: an urban style with rustic comfort.

CARSON'S FIVE FAVOURITE SUN PLANTS

If you have a garden with full sun, well-drained loam for soil and lots of water, then 90 per cent of gardeners hate you. Enjoy their jealousy and plant some of my favourite awe-inspiring plants.

1. **Double Flowering Tiger Lilies—** *Lilium lancifolium* This stunner has incredible double-petaled flowers atop seven-foot-tall stems.
2. **Globe Thistle—***Echinops ritro* Looks great even without flowers on it.
3. **Bearded Iris—***Iris germanica* The one plant that every garden should have for its unique assortment of colours.
4. **Lamb's Ear—***Lavendula angustifolia* Soft leaves in a delightful grey shade are irresistible and safe for small children.
5. **Black Eyed Susan—***Rudbeckia* There is nothing that can compare to a large clump of this easy-to-grow, cheerful flower.

DOs & DON'Ts

DON'T save a plant or tree if it's not in the right spot. Too often we get sentimental about a particular shrub or tree and try to design around it. People put plants in the wrong place all the time because they don't realize how that plant grows. You can drive down any street in North America and see an example of someone who has planted an evergreen too close to the foundation of their house and now it's blocking their windows. Always look for options in trying to save these plants, but be realistic: if its time to go then make the cut.

DO consult your local bylaws when deciding on an outdoor fireplace or chimenea. In some areas, they are perfectly acceptable. In others, there are restrictions as to how they are used. If it has a grill, for example, it may be considered a barbecue. In some municipalities, it isn't the fire that's the issue; it's the smoke. The law in this case allows for the fireplace as long as the smoke doesn't go into your neighbour's property. Don't assume that because a store sells it that you can use it. Check before you buy.

The new design plan divides the garden into four parts. One quadrant is dedicated to the new shed, another to a child's play structure, a third for a patio and dining area, and the fourth for the hottub. Beds full of perennials and shrubs link each area and act as a focal point when the couple looks out the kitchen window. The shed and swing set are placed on opposite ends of the garden to keep the space visually balanced, while the patio and spa remain alongside the

Plan

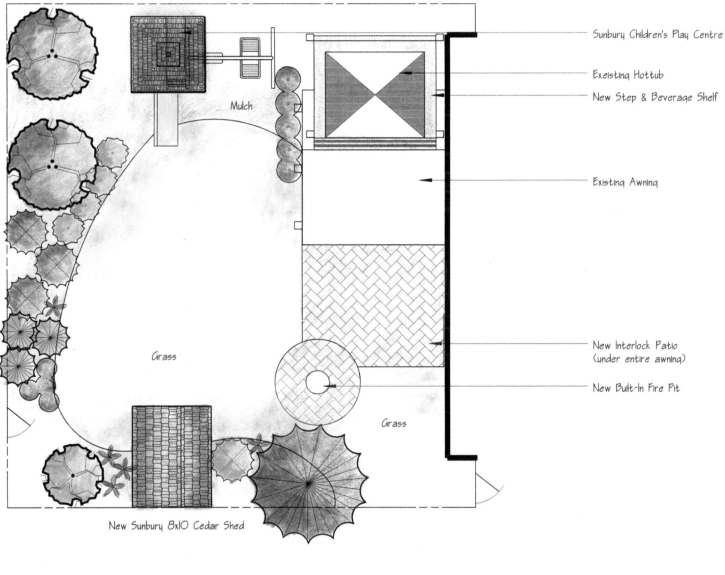

Sunbury Children's Play Centre

Exeisting Hottub

New Step & Beverage Shelf

Existing Awning

Mulch

Grass

New Interlock Patio
(under entire awning)

New Built-In Fire Pit

Grass

New Sunbury 8x10 Cedar Shed

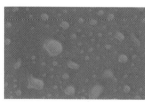

Yellow is introduced as the prominent colour in both the flowers and accessories: a subtle reminder of Catriona's back-to-back gold medals.

Materials

A multifunctional play structure is added for Greta to grow into. Even though there's a play area at a nearby school, Greta won't be old enough to use it for many years without supervision but with the new cedar swing and slide in the yard, she has a play area that Mom and Dad can supervise.

It is important to have materials that work well together. The new fire pit and interlock patio are made of one type of stone. Whenever possible, choose the same product line for all of your materials, but feel free to play with colour. Bricks with similar shapes and textures create a continuous look, while complementary but different colours can add depth to the same space by creating patterns.

Bart and Catriona needed a lot of storage, so a huge shed resembling a small cedar cabin replaced their outdated one. Homeowners are often afraid to bring large structures into a backyard because big items can overwhelm a small space. In this case, the shed is among the flowerbeds, so that plants and trees distract the eye and disguise the shed's depth.

house. The small seating area is doubled in size and the concrete slabs were replaced with interlock, which will allow for a large table and a new fire pit. The hottub, while staying in the same spot, gets new stairs for better access and several shelves. All of these elements surround a reseeded lawn, which keeps the backyard feeling open and spacious.

clockwise from top left:
Spiderwort—*Tranescatia 'Bilberry Ice'*
Bearded Iris—*Iris germanica 'Chinquapin'*
Lily—*Lilium hybrida 'Butter Pixie'*
Globe Thistle—*Echinops sphaerocephalus*

opposite:
Golden Ninebark—*Physocarpus opulifolius 'Dart's Gold'*

Catriona's wish list also included adding more bright flowers to her space. With a short season, growing perennials in Calgary can be difficult, but not impossible. Beds that are protected from the wind by the fence are the perfect spot to place some less hardy but sun-loving plant life. We gave Catriona a mix of shrubs and flowers that are sure to please but will also do well in the growing environment. We also amended the soil with a blend of equal parts of topsoil, sand and manure to help get her blooms on the fast track by providing them all of the necessary nutrients for vigorous growth.

The furniture for this space has to be tasteful enough for the city folk, but appropriate for a home on the range. Comfortable seating and occasional tables are ideal around the fire while a dining set is required for barbecues. The patio itself, although divided into two separate areas, has to be unified by the furniture. Dark colours are combined with bright accessories. Pieces need to be solid but refined enough to suit the urban locale. The furniture also needs to be durable, able to be hosed off when Greta spills ice cream or when Bart sits down to pull off his dirty cowboy boots.

The interior designer, Dean Debienne, evaluates his 'inspiration' for the new outdoor space.

Sometimes it is hard to make changes to our homes but Catriona and Bart realized that while their backyard wasn't meeting their needs, they had no idea of where to begin.

The formerly nondescript space out back became a garden that is everything this family was seeking. Bart has a new shed, big enough to hold his riding gear, including his dirty clothes, but not so large that he feels that the yard is crammed. Catriona gets her interlock stone patio, a spot for a fire and furniture ready to handle anything from board meetings to Silly Putty. And even though Greta couldn't say what she wanted, the play structure is a guaranteed hit. The swing set and slide are now quietly tucked into the corner waiting for the time when they will be used. It's safe and designed to keep her busy for the next 10 years.

Bart, Catriona and Greta may not have the home in the country they long for, but with some planning, they now have a little country in their home.

Refeathering the Nest

A time for refeathering the nest: reclaiming a backyard from sleepovers and soccer matches.

Sometimes it is easier to give up the yard to the kids. No stress about uprooted roses or a lawn worn thin; most parents just let their offspring play where no one can see the destruction. From threadbare to comfortably plush, a children's tattered play area is reclaimed.

No one will deny that Brad and Nancy love their children, John and Amy, but with one gone and the other on his way, it's time to take back the playground. Until now, the average-sized yard has been the domain of the kids and their friends, but Brad and Nancy remember the cute space that graced the house when they bought it 18 years ago. Once a perfect garden without the torn-up sod and half dead flowers, the backyard was a selling feature. Brad and Nancy are ready to restore the space to its former glory with a design created just for them.

opposite: *The small deck looks like an adult-sized playpen. Just large enough for a small set of wicker furniture, it will be rebuilt to meet Brad and Nancy's current needs.*

Looking like a cemetery for abandoned sporting equipment, this backyard is tired. Old railroad ties hold back empty perennial beds from encroaching on a lawn that has seen the soles of many teenage shoes. A shed that was once a playhouse sits forgotten in the corner, surrounded by basketball nets and golf clubs. The only adult influence is the small deck attached to the house. The quaint set of wicker furniture is an attempt at respectability in a yard that has been through it all.

Brad wants a low-maintenance garden that won't keep him from the golf course. Unfortunately, the perfect day for golfing also happens to be the best day for doing yard work, which means that this garden will get neglected in favour of tee times. Nancy wants a space that she can enjoy, even if it's just from the kitchen window. She wants to have people over and not be embarrassed by the mess. Nancy wants a backyard just like the ones in the magazines she's always reading.

DOs & DON'Ts

DON'T get sentimental about a backyard. Too often we leave our outdoor spaces exactly as they were when the kids were little. The old sand box and swing set have become permanent fixtures in some landscapes. Gardens, like homes, need to develop and change as your family grows. Plan landscaping that can evolve: the swing becomes your new perennial bed; the sandbox is the site of your future pond.

DO install big elements in a small garden, especially when it comes to useable space. People are afraid to put large patios or decks in small gardens because they worry that the yard will feel crowded. The exact opposite is true. When your guests have to cram onto the small deck—they feel crowded. Always go bigger. Think about how you want to use your garden and design accordingly. Never give up useable space for things like lawns and flowerbeds that are esthetic versus practical. Incorporate pots and planters if you feel that you need more colour on your new patio.

CARSON'S FIVE FAVOURITE SHADE PLANTS

I think of shade as a refuge from the sun. Shady places are calm and quiet, which is why I love them in cool colours: greens, blues, whites and even blacks.

1. **Peegee Hydrangea**
   —*Hydrangea paniculata* 'Grandiflora'
2. **Black Snakeroot or Bugbane**
   —*Cimicifuga racemosa*
3. **Applecourt Japanese Painted Fern**
   —*Athyrium niponicum* 'Applecourt'
4. **Brunnera**
   —*Brunnera macrophylla* 'Jack Frost'
5. **Lungwort or Bethlehem Sage**
   —*Pulmonaria saccharata*

This garden has to look good with little attention because it is going to be left alone most of the time.

The grass—as the highest maintenance item—has to go and with it, the railroad ties and all of the dead perennials. A new and larger deck replaces the old one. Going from a 12-by-12-foot deck to one that is 15 by 15 feet gives Nancy about 100 extra square feet of useable space, which translates to seating for at least 10 people instead of four. New storage, a bigger patio and plants that grow in the shade, round out the garden and give it shape. The pièce de résistance of this space is an incentive to keep Brad off the links and at home for at least some of the summer.

Plan

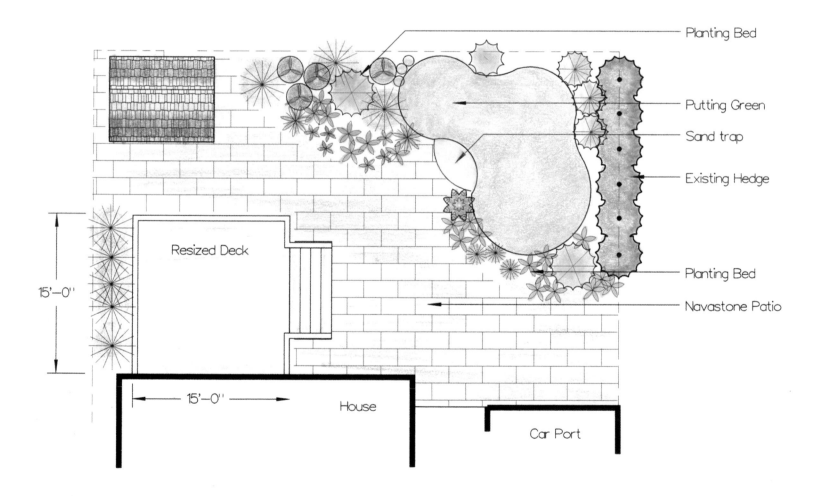

Materials

A four-hole putting green is the only thing that will keep Brad at home for some of the summer. New technology has created a surface, called synthetic grass, that is virtually maintenance-free, completely weatherproof and fade resistant. The only work required for this type of artificial sod will be to sweep off the leaves in the fall. Most companies will handle all of the installation, so you just have to decide on how many holes. Looking good as a focal point, this new feature will provide Brad hours of entertainment.

Originally chosen by Brad and Nancy as a durable yet attractive surface for the small pathway leading to the old deck, this paving stone is also ideal for creating more seating areas around the yard. A fashionable creamy salmon colour, the stones will be arranged in a geometric pattern of straight lines and square edges. It will act to counterbalance the freeform shapes of the flowerbeds and the putting green.

One other family member has a very specific need for this backyard. Abby, the family dog, currently does her business in the old flowerbeds, which works well for everyone. So even though we're keeping her private bathroom, the surface she is using will change. Cedar mulch is ideal for doggie clean up. There is no mud to track around and cedar also limits the ticks and fleas that would call love to call Abby home.

The plants in this garden are accessories with the two-fold purpose of looking good and giving the dog privacy. Therefore, they need to survive with minimal care and, though not the focal point, the flora would be missed if it wasn't there. Shrubs such as Hydrangea and perennials such as Daylilies, fill the empty spaces in this partial sun and shade garden and soften the hard elements like the shed and the patio.

clockwise from top:
Autumn Joy Sedum—*Sedum spectabile*
Dogwood—*Cornus alba 'Gouchaultii'*
Peegee Hydrangea—*Hydrangea paniculata*

opposite, clockwise from top left:
Japanese Spurge—*Pachysandra terminalis*
Euonymus—*Euonymus fortunei 'Canadale Gold'*
Daylily—*Hemerocalis 'Chicago Apache'*

Conservative in her own way, Nancy's new furniture should reflect her sensibilities. She got it right with her resin wicker furniture the first time but she didn't get enough of it. In addition to the original two chairs and loveseat, she now needs a table and a pair of loungers on the larger deck, a bench for the bottom of the steps and table and chairs on the new and bigger patio area. By combining Nancy's original pieces with other resin wicker and some durable teak, the space takes on that lived-in feeling. Designers call this shabby chic, but it really means mixing old with new to create a warm and intimate surrounding.

Ernst Hupel, the furniture consultant, and Carson decide what would work best beside the new putting green.

When children leave to start their own lives, many parents don't know what to do with their free time and space. In this case, Brad and Nancy regained the use of their yard. Redesigned and rebuilt, the new garden is perfect for adults to enjoy. Brad and Nancy's bigger and better deck has become the spot for red wine, antipasto and planning trips with friends. Although a little decadent, the putting green is a unique focal point where Brad and his buddies can work on their game and one day it might inspire Nancy to play too. Plenty of storage space in the new shed houses all of the old toys and equipment, ready for the yard sale next spring. A patio links the elements and the plants make everything look just right. The garden is now neat, orderly and absolutely charming, like its homeowners.

A Place to Play

From forgotten to fabulous,
a tired backyard is revived.
Ready for nights full of hockey,
hops and hickory barbecue sauce.

Rob and Julie bought their first home as an investment in an urban neighbourhood valued for its schools and parks. They knew that with some work, they could renovate the house, live in it for a few years and eventually sell it for a profit. With most of the renovating now complete, the only challenge remaining is the backyard.

Rob and Julie love to be outside. They use their small deck every morning for breakfast and again for dinner. Rob installed a television outside for watching hockey with his friends, even in November. They want a backyard that meets their needs, but is stylish enough to appeal to future buyers.

The design for this backyard has to accommodate large-scale entertaining. With so many friends from school just around the corner, the question is never "is there a party?" it's "what time is the party?"

The plan includes building a much larger deck—one that would take up two-thirds of the yard—with enough room for a large table and a separate seating area for watching hockey. Framing the yard is a collection of conifers.

The monochromatic colour scheme of lush greens is perfect to give the space shape and definition without visually overwhelming the small garden. In keeping with the idea of having a fun space, the remainder of the garden was inspired by the way Italians use small spaces for games of bocce and intimate gatherings. The back section of the garden therefore becomes the perfect place to build up an appetite.

Plan

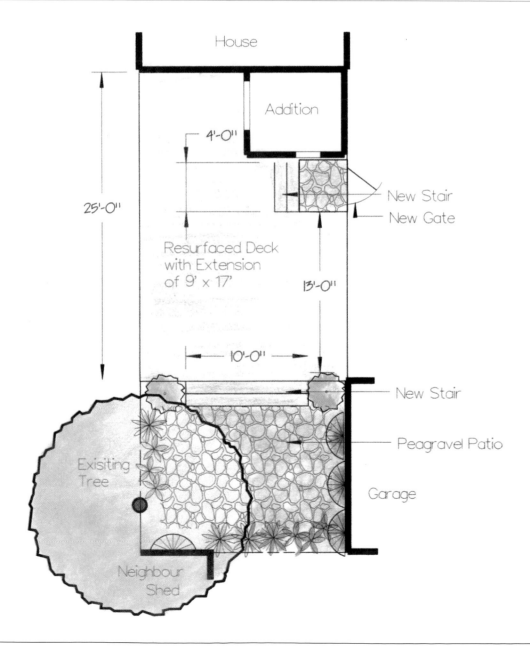

House

Addition

4'-0"

New Stair
New Gate

25'-0"

Resurfaced Deck
with Extension
of 9' x 17'

13'-0"

10'-0"

New Stair

Peagravel Patio

Garage

Exisiting
Tree

Neighbour
Shed

WHAT HEIGHT SHOULD MY DECK BE?

Too often I see people who have built great decks just below the height of their French doors. In principle fewer stairs seem like a great idea, and the convenience of having an outdoor living space just outside your kitchen is very appealing, but the truth is that you have put yourself completely on display for all of the other houses that share your backyard vista. Trust me on this one, lower is better unless you have a fantastic view of the lake or the city skyline. Privacy is very hard to create once the deck has been put in. Screens and planter boxes can only go so far. For your comfort, and that of your guests, consider a ground level deck or patio that takes advantage of the existing buildings, walls and fences.

Materials

Conical and spherical evergreens are chosen and planted together to give more interest. When planting, space these trees 24 to 36 inches apart, as measured from trunk to trunk. In time, the gaps will disappear as the shrubs begin to grow. Eventually, the different heights will create a wave effect that wraps the entire garden in an undulating band of green.

Taking inspiration from Italy, pea gravel was used as a versatile ground covering for low-maintenance spaces. With no watering, weeding, or feeding, pea gravel is much easier to look after than grass. It has only two drawbacks: unless you use a filter cloth underneath, weeds will easily grow through the small stones and the neighbourhood cats often confuse it with a litter box.

To give the yard an old-world feel, the garage wall is recovered with a stone alternative. To keep costs down, this man-made product is selected because it looks great and is easy to install. Lightweight concrete is ideal for indoor and outdoor applications and with several colours to choose from, the garage wall has become a focal point.

Julie likes monochromatic flowerbeds. What could be more perfect than an entire garden of a single colour in a few different shades? In a small space, the impact created by limiting to one or two plant families is much stronger than trying to mix and match. The genius to using only conifers is three-fold: you only have to buy one type of fertilizer, the plants can all be watered at the same time, and you only have to prune once a season.

Green, green and more green; this small garden will brim with evergreens.

below:
Mugho Pine—*Pinus mugo mugo*

clockwise from top left:
Pyramidal Yew—*Taxus cuspidata 'Clipped Cone'*
Boxwood—*Buxus 'Green Mound'*
Dwarf Hinoki False Cypress—*Chamaecyparis obtuse 'Nana Gracilis'*

Designer Suzanne Martin and Carson discuss all the new space on the deck.

Rough and rowdy and on a budget, Rob and Julie need furniture that can handle excitable sports fans and still look good when the in-laws visit. The new deck allows for a large table that seats at least eight and Rob and his buddies still have a space to watch the game. With resin club chairs and a propane deck heater, he can stay outside all the way to playoffs.

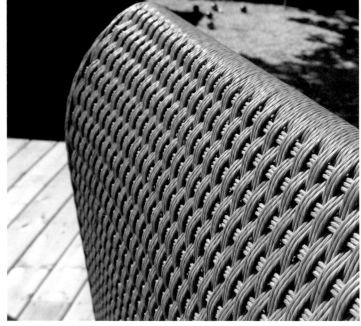

opposite: *The only request that Rob and Julie made was that the umbrella didn't stick out of the middle of the table. The nine-foot diameter umbrella has an extension arm that allows Rob and Julie to place the base off-to-the-side so that they never have to talk around a pole in the centre of their table.*

With the smell of steaks on the grill, several buddies playing bocce, and the sound of a game in the background, this garden is perfect for Rob and Julie and all of their friends with enough room for everyone on the large new deck. As far as putting the house up for sale, Rob and Julie may take their time, as they now have the backyard of

their dreams. When they do, this selling feature will be a highlight of the home.

The inspiration was Italy, and the garden feels like a courtyard in Sicily with its fieldstone walls and graveled floor. Gelato during the day and grappa at night, this garden was designed for a young couple that is enjoying life.

Ravished to Ravishing

A backyard that looks post-apocalyptic becomes reborn as a sanctuary for a family with teenagers.

There is nothing more devastating to a garden than a home renovation. Trucks, heavy materials in wheelbarrows and work boots just don't mix well with plants and grass. From rubble to radiant, this backyard is transformed into a space for outdoor living.

After spending time and effort overseeing the construction of a new kitchen and a family room addition on the back of their home, Sam and Rhonda are physically and emotionally exhausted from making design decisions. They want their 5,000-square-foot yard turned into a paradise and are willing to let someone else make all of the decisions. Sam and Rhonda just want all of the indoor and outdoor renovations finished.

Their wish list includes a patio to hold all of their kid's friends and greenery for Rhonda, who wants a view from her newly added kitchen window. Sam and Rhonda also hope to revive their grass to lure their children, young teens Andrew and Rebecca, away from the television and back outside.

They might as well have asked for the moon while they were at it.

And they wonder why the kids don't play in the yard anymore!?!

What was once a quaint yard with grass, a few flowerbeds and a single mature tree has become a dirt wasteland. Nothing remains of the lawn or the flowers since the renovation occurred. Now this depressing bowling alley only has fences on each side that emphasize the property's length. Even the shed, which may once have blended into the background, is now painfully obvious. Having a clean slate may be a landscaper's dream but working with this kind of devastation is a different story.

CARSON'S FIVE FAVOURITE HARDY PLANTS

Designed by nature to handle abuse, these plants are great for around soccer fields, dog runs and basketball courts. Dense and yet flexible, with or without thorns, these shrubs can take a beating and bounce right back.

1. **5-leaf Aralia—*Acanthopanax sieboldianus***
2. **Barberry—*Berberis thunbergi***
3. **Curly Willow—*Salix contorta***
4. **Red-twig or Siberian Dogwood —*Cornus alba* 'Sibirica'**
5. **Artic Willow—*Salix purpurea* 'Melanostchys'**

DOs & DON'Ts

DO be careful when considering putting in permanent structures like pools, putting greens and basketball courts. Most real-estate professionals will caution against adding something not easily removed, as it can affect the sale of your home. In this case, Sam and Rhonda live in a neighbourhood perfect for raising children, close to schools and parks. Anyone looking to move here will likely have kids of their own, so having the court in the back corner of the yard won't hurt the value of the house when it's time to sell.

DON'T plant evergreens is a straight line when trying to make a screen. Never in nature do trees grow in a perfect row. To create a naturalized effect, stage the trees in two lines. Bring every second tree forward so that it slightly overlaps the two behind. This way you'll get more privacy and it will look less like a row of soldiers and more like your very own forest.

Rhonda has garden envy. She loves the way her neighbour's space looks and wants several of the same plants in her own backyard.

opposite, left to right:
Highbush Cranberry—*Viburnum opulus*
Bloodgood Japanese Maple—*Acer palmatum*
Peegee Hydrangea—*Hydrangea paniculata*

Plan

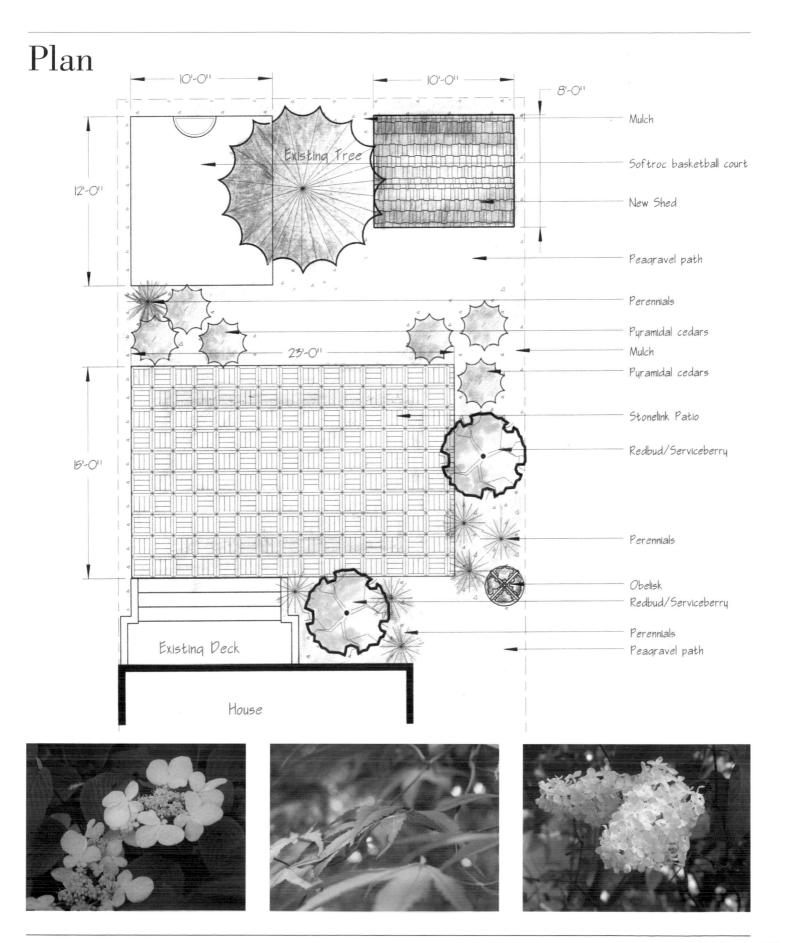

10'-0"

10'-0"

8'-0"

12'-0"

Existing Tree

Mulch

Softroc basketball court

New Shed

Peagravel path

Perennials

Pyramidal cedars

Mulch

Pyramidal cedars

23'-0"

Stonelink Patio

Redbud/Serviceberry

15'-0"

Perennials

Obelisk

Redbud/Serviceberry

Existing Deck

Perennials

Peagravel path

House

To break up the bowling alley, the garden will be divided horizontally. From the bottom of the steps, a new patio will be built across the width of the yard to draw the eye from side to side, not front to back. A collection of trees and shrubs will frame the patio and add vertical screening. The shed will stay in the same location but be replaced with a new model. Behind the shrubs and beside the shed will be a kid's space. Separated from the house and the patio, it will hopefully encourage them to come outside.

above: *Yews help screen and divide the yard because they grow in shaded areas and still stay dense.*

below: *The contrasting dark border emphasizes the perpendicular patio in the linear yard.*

Materials

Even though Sam and Rhonda thought grass was a good surface for their kids, this rubber composite material is a better choice. With several suppliers competing in the market, this product is readily available and cost efficient. By building a half-basketball court in the back corner of the yard, we hope to lure Andrew from the couch and where big brother goes, little sister is sure to follow. Not only soft, this flooring reduces the noise of a bouncing ball, so Andrew won't disturb the neighbours when he is out there for hours on end.

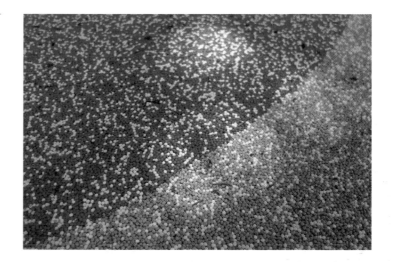

Natural flagstone is the most expensive product for a patio but this less expensive man-made product so closely resembles the real thing that most people can't tell the difference. Using rubber moulds, manufacturers are able to recreate the look of stone with concrete, at a fraction of the cost. Even the colours are chosen to fool the eye because they mimic the hues and tones found in nature.

The old shed may have been adequate but it was ugly, ugly, ugly! The new shed was chosen for its visual charm. Now, when Rhonda looks out the kitchen window, she sees a picture-perfect ginger-bread house, which hides all of the balls, bikes and hockey nets.

With a 70-year-old spruce tree casting shade over the yard for most of the day, plant selections were limited to those that can handle less light. The other consideration in this space was the basketball court. Without a way to stop the ball from landing in the flowers, plants have to be hardy enough to handle the abuse of rowdy games of hoops.

left: Hosta 'Blue Moon'—*Hosta*
top: Lady's Mantle—*Alchemilla mollis*
bottom: Berberis—*Berberis valdiviana*

On a simple base of 12-by-12-inch cement slabs, this rubberized surface is ideal for creating useable space at a low cost. Ideal for many applications and guaranteed to last, this product is perfect for stairs; around pools or in children's play areas.

The garden is said to be an extension of the home and the use of complementary furniture makes this happen. Guests should come from the front door through the house to a yard that is in harmony with the rest of the indoors. Dark rich wood in the kitchen cabinets is captured in the outdoor lounges and chairs while jewel-toned accessories emulates the rich red and terracotta paints on the family room walls. Seating areas designed for drinks and dining makes the patio multifunctional and allows Rhonda to plan for dinner parties that start with cocktails, move to the table for entrées and back to the lounge chairs for aperitifs.

Interior designer, Theresa Macdonell.

From a dreary yard to one cleverly divided, this space has been transformed into a picturesque garden from every angle. By playing with lines of sight and evergreen screens, visitors are greeted with dramatic vignettes. We created a yard that feels wider, but still maintains its depth by using horizontal elements across the garden. Once renovation weary, the backyard has been revived as an outdoor extension of the house.

The tones in the cushions and accents are rich and vivid. The stone patio looks and feels sumptuous and textural. The furniture is ready for relaxing and entertaining while the kids are blissfully occupied in their teenage appropriate area off in the corner.

The garden feels like it was always meant to be there—the sign of good design.

A Place for Everyone

A boring yard in the burbs gets some much-needed TLC: making a space for the young and young at heart.

Life doesn't end when you have children and you shouldn't lose the use of your backyard to a bunch of toys. A well-designed garden should be an extension of a home with separate rooms for separate functions where everything has its own place.

Jason and Stacy are the proud parents of Cameron and Julia—and their dog, Rags. Family has been the focus in their lives for the last few years and with the purchase of a new and bigger house, having a backyard that works for everyone is now a priority. For them, days are about playtime and pandemonium, but their nights are a time free from children, perfect for entertaining old friends and playing board games. Their ideal garden does it all and easily changes from a space for the kids to a place for Mom and Dad.

A dilapidated deck, a yard full of grass and a much-used swing set are the only items found in a very large piece of land. Not nearly full, this rectangular garden has unrealized potential with more than 5,000 square feet of space.

The biggest challenge in this space will be to fulfill Jason's wish of less grass. In a backyard this big, most people throw down grass because it's an easy design solution and you can usually fill a large area at a low cost. This isn't always the best answer as Jason spends several hours per week cutting, mowing, weeding and watering a patch of sod. Stacy and Julia's request for the new yard is the inclusion of lots of flowers. Without any character, this plain suburban yard needs an infusion of life. It needs to emulate the rest of the house; neat and orderly but at the same time filled with colour and activity.

Having a swing set beside the deck may keep the children close, but it won't allow for much peace and quiet.

opposite: *To give Mom, Dad, Julia and Cameron their own space, the garden will be divided into three parts; adult, child and a transition area in between. In backyards where there is plenty of freedom, having separate rooms is easily accomplished with simple techniques such as different surface materials or even dividers like a fence or hedge.*

Plan

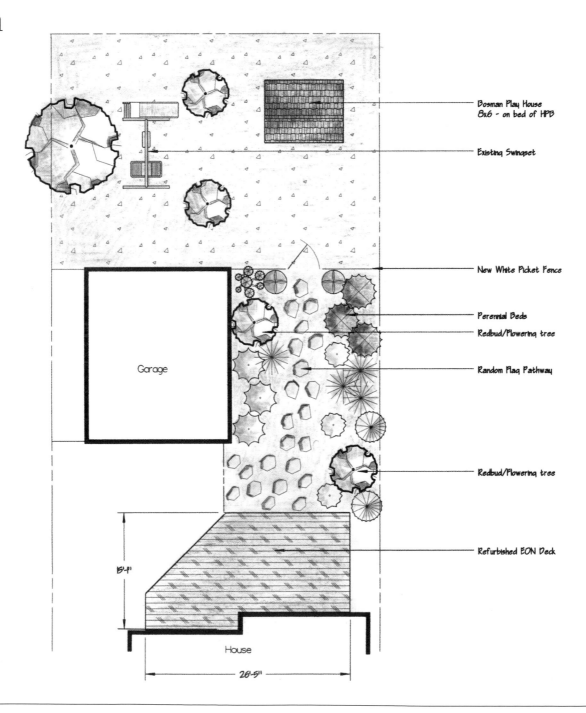

Bosman Play House
8x6 - on bed of HPB

Existing Swingset

New White Picket Fence

Perennial Beds

Redbud/Flowering tree

Random Flag Pathway

Redbud/Flowering tree

Refurbished EON Deck

Garage

House

15'-4"

26'-5"

Areas with specific purposes are more clearly defined.

Moving the swing back and adding a white picket fence between it and the house, creates an outdoor playroom designed to hold all of the balls, trucks and doll sets. There also needs to be a focal point at the back of the yard that would make the view interesting from the house. Something large and attractive, the focal point should work towards the idea that this space is for play.

The space formerly occupied by the swing now becomes a transition area full of beautiful flowers and shrubs: A perfect spot for Julia and Stacy to share with all of the butterflies that will now visit.

The area near the house designated for the adults is also in need of a makeover. Although the deck is beginning to rot, it is only the surface of the deck that is damaged. The size and scale of the structure is good, so keeping the space relatively the same makes everyone happy and is most cost effective. The deck is resurfaced with material made from recycled plastics, which requires little maintenance. Jason and Stacy won't have time to spend on staining or sanding with all of the entertaining they plan to be doing.

The rectangular garden will be divided into three separate areas; adult, child and a transition space in between.

Designating the back of the yard as a children's play area was a strategic choice. For safety, everything would remain visible from the deck but a buffer zone for noise was created, benefitting both the playing children and the resting adults.

Luann Bryan and Carson making planting decisions.

DOs & DON'Ts

DO plant sun loving perennials under young trees. In optimum growing conditions, a deciduous tree will take about 15 years before it provides any shade to a space. The life of most perennials is much shorter then that. Slowly transition your garden from plants that require full sun, to ones suited for sun and part-shade, and finally to those for full-shade as the tree grows and blocks out more light.

DON'T place children's play structures immediately beside the family space; allow some separation between areas designed for rest and ones designed for rowdy play. We all know how hard it is to keep kids in one spot, but as long as young children are clearly visible, why not let them have some freedom in the backyard? Create a designated place just for them, free of danger and parental influence.

DO use indoor plants in your outdoor containers. Tropical plants make excellent additions to planter boxes and on patios in glazed pots. You can treat them like annuals and dispose of them at the end of the season, or for extended flowering, find a sunny spot in your home and winter them there.

Materials

An adorable children's playhouse becomes the focal point at the back of the yard. Toys may be colourful, but they're not something that your guests want to look at. With complementary colours, working windows and a Dutch door, this pint-sized palace is ideal for rainy days and sleepovers.

Replacing most of the sod with mulch allows Julia and Cameron to have an area free of mud and grass stains. The use of mulch in a children's area is excellent for several reasons: the relatively soft surface will compact with children running back and forth on it, it absorbs moisture and prevents mud, it also keeps weed seeds from reaching the soil below. The only down side is that the wood chips will eventually degrade and Stacy and Jason will have to replace them every few years, but at a minimal cost.

The current wooden deck is beginning to show its age and splinters have become a major concern for Jason and Stacy, as they expect to spend many summers barefoot around the kiddie pool. A wood alternative was chosen to resurface the deck in a beautiful cedar colour. Available at most hardware, lumber or box stores, this product is weather resistant; it won't fade, split, crack or rot. With railings, balusters and deck boards available in the same colours and materials, every exposed part of the old structure is replaced from the base up, creating something that lasts a lifetime and requires absolutely no care or maintenance.

Even though Stacy and Julia requested several different types of flowers, ensuring that they had gardens that required little work was crucial. Full-sun all day long made it very important to choose shrubs and flowers that were drought tolerant. The addition of a pair of trees will eventually provide some relief from the heat, but until then, the space still needs to be appealing. Although most plants require some work, the selected plants need less.

clockwise from top left:
Variegated Pagoda Dogwood—*Cornus alternafolia variegata*
Midnight Wine Weigela—*Weigela florida*
Stella d'Oro Daylily—*Hemerocallis*

Family-friendly furniture should to be resilient enough to handle the spills from dinner and more sophisticated than the white plastic alternative. Jason and Stacy want to make their friends sans children to feel at home in this space, so furniture colours and styles must be inviting to them too. The furniture must also be able to handle all of the elements, as bringing it in during a storm isn't likely to happen with this busy family.

Having a second seating area, solely designed for the children, gives Cameron and Julia a perfect spot for crafts or tea parties. Using furniture that is fun and colourful, but inexpensive, allows the imagination to take over and Mom

doesn't have to worry about it getting marked or scuffed. By placing this space behind the charming white picket fence, all of the mess is hidden.

Jillian Jeffery and Carson survey Jillian's furniture choices.

CHOOSING OUTDOOR FURNITURE

When looking for outdoor furniture, be prepared to make an investment. There are as many styles of chairs and tables for your deck as there are for your dining room. With so much selection, be realistic about what you need your furniture to do for you. Is it more then just as place to eat your steak and potatoes? Do you plan to have guests over? Will you have time to care for each piece? Do you plan to put the furniture away at the end of fall? In addition to these important questions, you should also measure the space before your start to shop. Make sure that the table you choose allows for at least four feet of free space on each side. With your guests and the chairs they are sitting on, you will find that the four feet rapidly disappears.

Creating an outdoor space for your children doesn't mean that you have to sacrifice the yard. In this case, everyone gets a little spoiled in a garden designed to be both practical and beautiful.

Julia and Cameron get the ultimate area just for them with plenty of room for the old swing set, all of the toys and the new playhouse. The back of the yard has now become their domain instead of the unused space it once was. Hours and hours will be spent tiring themselves out before dinner in the pursuit of absolutely nothing significant.

A white picket fence separates the bedlam from the rest of the quaint garden full of flow-ering perennials and easy-to-care-for shrubs. A bench becomes the perfect spot to stop, rest and read a book.

Jason and Stacy will be the envy of their friends as the newly resurfaced deck promises many nights of great food and great entertaining, separate from the clutter of the children's playthings.

Jason, Stacy, Julia, Cameron and even the dog, now have a backyard designed for a family who wants to spend their summer days together but also perfect for remembering what life was like before the kids.

143

Suburban Elegance

From totally overpowered to perfectly proportionate; a monolithic home gets a colossal backyard makeover.

Suburban homes seem to be getting bigger and bigger. Unfortunately, the lots don't appear to be growing with them. As a result, trying to create a balanced landscape for a gigantic home on a small plot of land can be a design challenge. In this case, grass makes way for a massive stone patio, all in the name of progress.

Abdol and Maryam love large spaces, which is why they decided to move to the suburbs five years ago. They wanted a large house and they bought one that is 5,000 square feet. They also got a backyard that looks directly into their neighbour's swimming pool. So for the last five years, Abdol and Maryam have stayed inside.

Now, their home is filled with treasures from their travels around the world and they need more space. They want to take advantage of their neglected garden for entertaining and barbecuing. They're ready to expand into a yard that is as customized as their home.

Ordinarily, garden design is only limited by the creativity of the designer. In this case, however, there is only one solution for creating a space for Abdol and Maryam. They need a very large patio in proportion to the size of the back wall of the house. To be balanced with the home, the patio should span from corner to corner and be as wide as at least three quarters of the height of the house. The new patio is more than 1,000 square feet and since the yard slopes towards the back of the property a retaining wall is required to manage the elevation change. While building this helicopter-landing pad is a large undertaking, it's not the toughest part of the design. The greatest challenge is privacy. Maryam is adamant that whatever is installed looks good from both sides and doesn't feel like a wall as she doesn't want her neighbours to be offended.

Plan

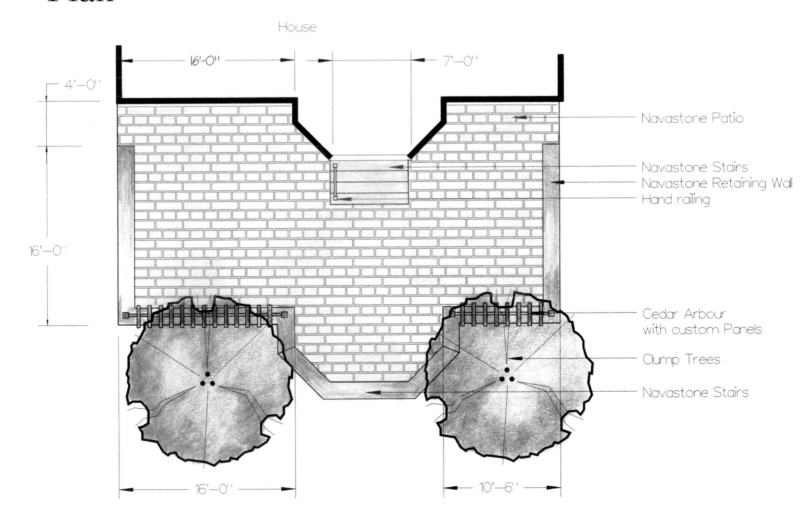

With such a small stretch of grass attached to a very large house, the backyard seems completely out of scale. Other than the wood fence that surrounds the property, there is nothing to visually balance the two-and-a-half storeys of grey brick and siding. Unfortunately, while it encloses the space, the fence doesn't provide privacy from the neighbour's aboveground swimming pool. When they moved, Abdul planted a row of shrubs and trees in hopes that they would one day break up the view. Five years later, they are only half way there.

The other noticeable component of Abdol and Maryam's backyard is the placement of the barbecue and the dining set. Without a patio, guests must sit in the grass and weeds.

Uneven lawn is probably not the most ideal base to put your outdoor dining furniture on. The best surfaces for tables are solid and stable; definitely not grass.

DOs & DON'Ts

DON'T underestimate how large to build your patio or deck. The absolute minimum for a table that seats four people is a 10-by-10-foot space. Most homes need a surface at least 15 by 15 feet to hold a table, a barbecue and all of your guests. Too often, we create small seating areas in favour of large lawns. Always plan for a bigger patio or deck than you think you need—we all find a way to fill it.

DON'T rely on plants for screening. Occasionally, there are examples of a perfect cedar wall that acts as a privacy barrier. Most times, the hedges are not so rosy. Dead at the bottom, or sparse with brown sections, living screens require a lot of maintenance. Use permanent solutions like lattice or Plexi-glass to create a year-round barrier. Once in place, plants can be added. This way, even if the plant struggles, you will always have your privacy.

With a patio this large, there was a lot of gravel used for the base; equal to 27 yards, two dump trucks, or 134 wheel barrow loads (but who's counting?).

PLANNING YOUR DECK'S SIZE

How do we know what the proper proportions of our decks and patios should be so that they work with the scale of our homes? There are as many answers for this question as there are materials to build with. My general rule of thumb is that the depth of your patio should be at least two-thirds the height of the wall it is attached to. If your home is a bungalow, then plan to use the entire height of the wall as your measurement. The width of your deck can be variable and still look good. In most cases, I tell homeowners to use the entire length of the wall you are building on as your measurement for the width. Sometimes this is very large, but for most backyards, the patio becomes the only useable space in the yard, so having more is always better.

Materials

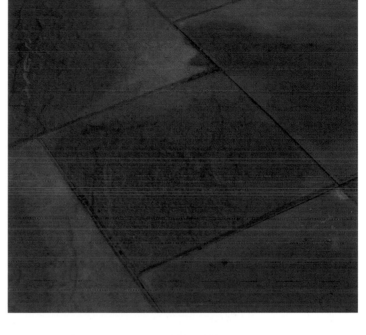

This patio stone was chosen for three reasons. Its matte finish complements the hues of the brick and siding without competing with the different tones of grey. The dark shade provides a visual anchor since it frames any furniture on the patio and lends an understated elegance. While it looks similar to a natural flagstone, it's a fraction of the cost.

opposite: *To solve Maryam's privacy dilemma, custom screens were built using cedar and Plexi-glass. With a milky, acid-wash finish, each panel feels light and fresh and although opaque, sunlight and shadows shine through. A Catalpa tree is planted behind the larger screen, so that the leaves create a spectacular reflection when the sun rises behind it in the early morning. The added bonus for Maryam's neighbour is the privacy they get while swimming in their pool.*

This retaining wall system called Hadrian's Stone is made up of only one size of brick. By cutting, twisting and flipping each stone to create intricate combinations, this wall is not only beautiful; it's one-of-a-kind. The grey colour of the wall works well with the flagstone and the house, which is important because the three materials are all different. When in doubt, always try to use one type of product in an area, but if you have to mix, then try to stay in the same colour palette. This creates unity in the space.

This garden was more about relocating the plants than replacing them. The original specimens were evenly spaced and staggered in a larger bed, so that the garden no longer looked like it was holding up the fence. Then a few perennials and shrubs were added to create plant beds with interest and colour.

opposite:
Catalpa—*Catalpa bignoniodis*

clockwise from top right:
Shrub Rose—*Rosa hybrida 'Knock Out'*
Cutleaf Smooth Sumac—*Stephanandra incisa 'crispa'*
Globe Cedar—*Thuja occidentalis 'Little Giant'*

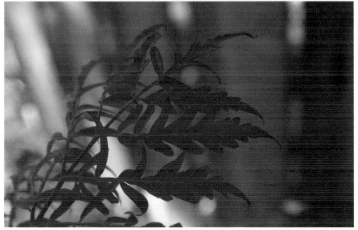

With all of the grey tones in the building materials, the furniture had to be something special so that it would stand out. It needed to be bright and fresh to keep the garden from looking monochromatic. The furniture also needed to blend with the contemporary feel of the space.

The large patio surface was designed to have two distinct sections: a dining area with a new barbeque and a large table and a lounge area with a propane fireplace and comfortable outdoor seating, including a sofa. Abdol and Maryam can now have private moments together behind the new screens.

Theoretically, designing gardens for new homes should be easy. Most spaces are blank slates, waiting for someone to make a decision. Unfortunately, blank slates are actually the hardest to design, since most new homes haven't developed their own character. One day, architectural companies will include the yards and plants with their plans for homes. They will design for the big picture, not each unit individually. In a perfect world, we would never move into neighbourhoods that have nothing but huge houses, large lawns and a few token trees.

To work with their large home, Abdol and Maryam wanted something grand. They chose

their home for its size, so the landscape design needed include elements that were proportionate. The simple use of a very large patio with screens solved their design dilemma and now the house and the yard feel complete as if one company designed both.